# X IN THE TICKSEED

# X
## IN THE
# TICKSEED

poems

ED FALCO

Louisiana State University Press
Baton Rouge

Published by Louisiana State University Press
lsupress.org

LSU Press Paperback Original

DESIGNER: Michelle A. Neustrom
TYPEFACE: Calluna, text; Avenir Next, display

COVER PHOTOGRAPH: *Waiting*, by Russ Morris.

Grateful acknowledgment is made to the editors of the following publications, in which the poems listed first appeared, sometimes under different titles: "X on Big Bass Lake," *32 Poems;* "Essay: On Tolstoy's 'The Death of Ivan Ilyich'" and "The Ruined Garden," *American Journal of Poetry;* "Essay: On Artemisia Gentileschi's *Judith Slaying Holofernes*" and "Essay: On Frank O'Connor's 'Guests of the Nation,'" *Gettysburg Review;* "As a Storm Approaches" and "Narcissus," *Hampden-Sydney Poetry Review;* "Amazing Machine the Body," *New South;* "X & the Spider" and "X on Fear & Joy," *Potomac Review;* "Essay: On Delacroix's *The Shipwreck of Don Juan*," "Three Transmutations of a Memory," "Three Views of a Lake," and "X's Shocked Heart," *Puerto del Sol;* "Girl on a Rooftop," *Smartish Pace;* "A Few Words to a Young American Killed in the Tet Offensive," "Essay: On Jay DeFeo's *The Rose*," "In the Kentucky Mountains," "X & Death," "X at 70, a Walk in the Woods," and "X in the Tickseed," *Southern Review.*

LIBRARY OF CONGRESS CATALOGING-IN-PUBLICATION DATA

Names: Falco, Edward, author.
Title: X in the tickseed : poems / Ed Falco.
Description: Baton Rouge : Louisiana State University Press, 2024. | "LSU Press
    Paperback Original"—Title page verso.
Identifiers: LCCN 2023035243 (print) | LCCN 2023035244 (ebook) | ISBN 978-0-8071-
    7920-8 (paperback) | ISBN 978-0-8071-8193-5 (epub) | ISBN 978-0-8071-8194-2 (pdf)
Subjects: LCGFT: Poetry.
Classification: LCC PS3556.A367 X56 2024 (print) | LCC PS3556.A367 (ebook) |
    DDC 811/.54—dc23/eng/20231005
LC record available at https://lccn.loc.gov/2023035243
LC ebook record available at https://lccn.loc.gov/2023035244

for Judy Bauer

# CONTENTS

# X IN THE TICKSEED

# X & the Spider

## 1.

This morning X kills a small black spider in the kitchen
      Sink and the insignificance of its squiggly, rudimentary
Life causes him a brief pause, a second's momentary
      Reflection.

      It's not just that little will be undone in this spider's
Absence, that not a single blessed thing of import will
      Change; rather, it's the thought of death's arbitrary
      Nature.

## 2.

One moment this spider scurries toward sun and glistening
      Water, a tiny bubble of moisture on bright stainless
Steel that seems to vibrate in the open kitchen window's
      Light

      And the next moment it's gone, erased, nothing
Remains but a smudge which X quickly washes
      Away before going on about his everyday
      Business.

## 3.

Around X the countless stars soar and shout their cosmic
      Noise, their immense cataclysmic tumult
Rollicking through the infinite and towering
      Beyond

      Through endless stretches of nothing through
Vast seas of everything brilliant exploding crashing
      Destroying and creating, all of it going on
      Forever.

# X on Big Bass Lake

## 1.

Because mosquitoes on land are driving X crazy, he takes the canoe
        Out onto Big Bass Lake and ties up to a tree half submerged off-
Shore. He slips inside the tube of his sleeping bag and huddles under
        Thwarts.

        One ear pressed to the thin aluminum skin of the canoe: water
Rushes past in a quick current, the whoosh of it a lullaby, a soft
        Song whispered throughout the night, under the stars' scattered
            Blaze.

## 2.

Above X a steady breeze keeps the little beasts at bay: the miserable blood-
        Suckers on shore dipped tiny beaks through his itchy skin for a quick
Sip. Out on the water the lake rocks him close to sleep, the wind
        Soothes

        And the stars, the vast, inconceivable, bright immensity of all those
Points of light pierce the black mask of Nothing, under which X is so
        Small he feels himself a faint spark in a great all-encompassing
            Peace.

## 3.

When he dreams he dreams of home and the shed roof at night on a quiet
        Street in Brooklyn, where he once focused a telescope on the moon's
Craters—only now he steps off the edge and flies over the city's million
        Rooftops

        Up so high the whole island of Manhattan in its dress of bright lights takes
Shape beneath him, and then the Eastern Seaboard and the North American
        Continent and the planet itself as he rises higher into the unbounded
            Night.

# Girl on a Rooftop

Girl on a Brooklyn rooftop in moonlight.
        Her waltz-length white nightgown flurried
                By gusts of wind off the East River.
One foot rests on the head of a gargoyle.
        The boy watching from his bedroom window is still unsoiled
                By lust, greed, ambition, anger, or terror.
He's a child who awoke one night and went to his bedroom window
        Where he saw a girl in a nightgown on his neighbor's rooftop
                The instant before she dropped to the sidewalk
Her waltz-length white nightgown swooping ever after through moonlight.

Fire season in the West
        Feels like the whole country is burning.
                I'm tired all the time and sleep comes with great difficulty.
Men are rousted out of bed, papers are demanded.
        The donkey in my neighbor's fields
                Screams as if being molested.
Goldfinches slash yellow flames to the flashy pink petals of a cherry tree.
        Refugees and their children are drowning.
                Sleep comes only with great difficulty.

There must have been stories, though no one told me
        A boy whose sensitivity
                Worried his working-class family.
In memory her hair is dark and riffled by the wind.
        Her gown is white against faint stars in a black background
                A bright full moon gazing overhead.
The blue slate sidewalk below her is out of sight.
        It's late, past midnight
                The lights are out in my parents' bedroom.
Though they wouldn't tell me, they must have known her story.

She has become for me an image and a mystery.
        The world goes on daily in its brutal way

Through gorgeous columns of light and shade.
The executioner's children eat well and prosper.
        The murdered are felled and drop and assume grotesque postures
            Spilled along city streets or remote mountain valleys
While she remains always on the edge of that rooftop
        Looking out over night and the sleeping city
            On the verge forever of slipping off into the moonlight
Like love and suffering and sorrow and beauty.

## The Ruined Garden

We counted the silence between breaths and waited.
       Soon, we were told, very soon.
Her slivered body weighted to stillness, her searching eyes blind.
       Four of her five children in a circle around her
The girls holding her hands, the boys at her feet.

What would we find
       Could we step behind her shuttered eyes?

       A garden in summer, her husband at her side
Holding a dirt-crusted trowel, and she with a flowering lily
       Cupped in the palms of her outstretched hands.

When I was still a boy and the two of them would live forever:
       Sun bright on our green, precisely mown lawn
The bright array of their tenderly attended garden—
                      The hen and chicks
The bleeding hearts
           Purple salvia
                 Ornamental grasses
       Angel's breath and row upon row of marigolds
Zinnias, day lilies, and more, and more than I can remember.

       And this: the morning I helped her plant
           A row of bright red flowers
                 Poppies maybe
Delicate red petals and black center.
                   A child in my mother's arms
After the sky darkened and clouds
       Tumbled over roofs, then thunder, lightning
A screeching wind an outburst of hail and I cried
       For the lost morning's work
          For the garden ruined
            For the red petals stripped

The plants beaten
To the ground.

Her lips at my ear, whispering to her child:
"There's no need for tears:
Everything's only beautiful for a little while."

## After Your Call

Your voice is weak on the phone
      So far away, so much distance
            So many years undone and undoing.

You employ a glib good humor
      Tell me there's no sense in worrying
            All will go on as it always has

While storm clouds here are dark and fast moving.
      Wind bellows its brute song as it bends trees
            In an eerie pre storm light.

In my yard wild with summer greenery
      As birds screech and dart branch to branch
            For every borrowed day

I thank the darkening sky, the clouds roiling lower
      The diminishing light and chill wind
            The lightning split and blast of thunder.

## A Short Essay about Heartbreak

It doesn't happen all at once. Years later
      A dozen years after the drinking killed you
While I'm in line at Starbucks waiting for coffee

I remember a visit when you turned in early.
      You're there, fragile as ever
Looking tired, closing the guest-room door behind you.

Now I know you had a bottle in the room.
      I see you sitting on the edge of the bed
In the dark, drinking in secret, and there it is again

Years later, heart like a wound still throbbing as it heals.

## A Short Essay about Illusions

Your house looked lovely
      Neatly arranged
But everything in it fell apart
      At a touch.

The lovely accent chests
      Propped up on broken legs
The lamps balanced on their bases
      The credenza with doors
That fell off if opened.

A stranger couldn't see
      How fragile it all was
That house where you lived.

# X & the Boy

A boy alone somewhere sulking beneath
      Skin, in the heart's every beat, every
Sputter: a shy child, eyes on the ground, beaten
      Down

      By a father enraged at a recalcitrant
World bent on his daily humiliation, refusing
      Respect, or even allowing a decent
          Living.

2.

The boy bears the backhand of his father's anger
      Still. Decades after the old man's heart at last
Failed, the child waits alone in a murky
      Cellar.

      Toward the despairing child, the man feels
Tenderness. He's made peace with his troubled
      Father long ago. His life was a long
          Struggle.

3.

Some nights X takes his child by the hand, walks
      Beneath the night's white moon and burning
Stars, does his best to explain their shared
      Blessings.

      X counts out grace and still the boy sulks
Wounded by every unearned blow, every
      Curse rained down that still he can't
          Forgive.

# X & Death

1.

X has spent a lifetime worrying about dying. He
  Reminds himself of a child who starts
Crying upon entering a gaudy amusement
  Park:

  All the rides! The Parachute Jump! The Ferris
Wheel! The wild roller coasters! Plus all the other
  Attractions! The Haunted Mansion! The Mirrored
   Maze!

2.

"I don't want to go home yet!" the child cries at the ticket
  Gate. "Please," he asks his mother, "can we please
Stay?" When his mother explains that they've only just
  Arrived

  The child is not placated. He cries and cries: he's
Stuck on what he knows is coming, when the rides
  Stop spinning and the lights go out and it's time to go
   Home.

3.

X crouches beside a shallow stream and looks at his
  Reflection above the pebbles: his hair has turned
Gray and under his eyes there are dark circles. Above X
  White

  Clouds drift lazily through an ocean-blue sky;
Below him the stream murmurs a lullaby and X leans down
  Kisses the moving water as if it were a departing
   Lover.

## Essay: On Jay DeFeo's *The Rose*

It's the texture, thick three-dimensional layers turning paint
   Into sculpture, that distinguishes Jay DeFeo's *The Rose.*
That and its massive size and weight—and the legend. *The Rose*
   Consumed DeFeo for eight years, while she lived on Fillmore
Street in San Francisco with her husband, Wally Hedrick. Together
   They entertained the poets, artists, and musicians of the Beat
Generation, going together one evening to hear Allen Ginsberg's
   First reading of "Howl," at the Six Gallery. Kerouac, Ferlinghetti
Neal Cassady, and Gary Snyder were also there.

Between 1958 and 1966, in those years with American culture
   Convulsing, casting off the conservatism of the '50s, moving
On from black-clad, finger-snapping beatniks to the long-haired
   Free-love hippies of the Haight, DeFeo worked and reworked
And worked over *The Rose,* layering paint on paint, shaping pigment
   With a palette and trowel until the canvas, a foot thick and nearly
Eleven feet high, weighed more than a ton and filled her apartment's
   Bay window, blocking out light where she sat on a scrapings-
Covered stool to contemplate what she was creating.

Jay's friend, the artist and filmmaker Bruce Conner, believes DeFeo
   Would have never quit work on *The Rose* had she not been
Evicted from her apartment. He filmed the removal, which necessitated
   Knocking out the wall around the bay window, laying the painting
Down, crating it, and lowering it to the street with a forklift. He believes
   Jay, at that point in her life with *The Rose,* was half-mad
With obsession—and the lead-based white paint didn't help. He took a
   Picture of her sitting on the ledge of the blasted-out window
Looking down at the street as if she might jump.

In 1959, early in her work on *The Rose,* DeFeo was one of two women
   In *Sixteen Americans,* an exhibit at MOMA that included Jasper
Johns, Ellsworth Kelly, Robert Rauschenberg, Frank Stella, and Louise
   Nevelson, as well as Wally Hedrick. The catalog

Has a picture of *The Rose,* described as an "unfinished oil painting
   Begun in 1958." No one could have known she would work on her
Unfinished oil painting for another seven years and on almost nothing
   Else, that *The Rose* would overwhelm her, and that she wouldn't
Stop working on it until she had no other choice.

*The Rose* wasn't exhibited until 1969. After that, it was installed in a room
   At the San Francisco Art Institute, where her friend Fred Martin was
Dean. In need of conservation, it was covered with plaster and chemicals
   And eventually wound up hidden behind a false wall, where it
Remained for 21 years. Before DeFeo's death in 1989, she told Leah Levy
   That she was having a vision. This is what she said she saw, while gazing
Directly over Levy's head: "I'm in another life and I'm walking in a museum
   And I come upon *The Rose,* and I see someone looking at it, and I walk
Up to them and nudge them and say, 'I did that.'"

I first saw *The Rose* in 2013, at the Whitney's *Jay DeFeo: A Retrospective.*
   Against a black wall, in a metal frame, by itself in a dark room
The painting glowed, light emanating out from its center as if it were itself
   A form of life. I thought of the artist alone in her apartment, scraping
And painting for eight years, while the changing world spun all around her.
   I thought of what Fred Martin wrote of Jay DeFeo and *The Rose*
The artist and her painting: "And you made a space of wings whence your soul
   Might look out. . . . All this, that for you and for us there be radiance."

## Essay: On Artemisia Gentileschi's *Judith Slaying Holofernes*

Artemisia would have known Caravaggio's *Judith Beheading Holofernes*
  Caravaggio being a friend of her father's.
In Caravaggio's painting, Holofernes, bearded, muscular, looks up at nothing
  In shock and paralyzed while Judith's sword slices
Neatly through his neck, as if his brawny flesh were soft as butter.
  Judith leans back from the mess, not a touch of blood on her flawless
Skin or sheer white blouse fitted to emphasize the fullness of her breasts.
  She appears distressed at the harsh unpleasantness of her work
But resolved to push on regardless.

Painters of that era knew the story from the Book of Judith: when the Assyrian
  General Holofernes besieges the city of Bethulia, Judith
Dons her most enticing garments, does up her hair, and enters the enemy camp
  Feigning to be a traitor, offering the Assyrians information
That will assure their victory. Holofernes, taken by Judith's beauty and hoping
  To seduce her, invites her to dine with him. Judith
Accepts, plies him with wine, and when he's too drunk to effectively resist
  She cuts off his head, hides it in a wicker basket
And returns triumphant to her people.

Artemisia's Judith is not nearly as delicate, fair, and preciously feminine
  As Caravaggio's. Unlike, also, Cristofano Allori's Judith
In *Judith with the Head of Holofernes,* whose striking beauty stares out at you
  From darkness, the general's head dangling delicately from her hand.
Artemisia's Judith, in contrast, has rolled up her sleeves, her dress slipped down
  Off one shoulder as she works to draw the sword through Holofernes's
Neck, blood splattered everywhere, spilling over three stacked mattresses
  As her handmaid struggles to keep Holofernes down
Judith's face a mask of contempt.

Caravaggio, Allori, Botticelli and others, all men—their paintings explored
    The biblical tale: Judith, the beautiful Israelite woman
And Holofernes, the brutal Assyrian general. Artemisia had her own story:
    Raped at seventeen by Agostino Tassi, a traveling artist hired
By her father to continue her education, Artemisia and her father brought
    Charges against him, and Artemisia endured a seven-month trial
That included torture—ropes tied around her fingers like thumbscrews to ensure
    Her honesty. When the cords tightened she cried "It's true! It's true! It's true!"
As Tassi, untouched, denied the accusations.

Though he was found guilty and sentenced to two years in prison, Tassi
    Served no time, favored as he was by Pope Paul V.
Artemisia, who was not born into wealth and didn't have Tassi's connections
    Went on anyway to a distinguished career. Propelled only by grit and genius
She asserted herself as one of the Italian Baroque's great artists.
    It's Artemisia's character you see in Judith as she holds Holofernes
Down and saws at his neck. In one version of the painting
    Judith wears a bracelet that depicts the goddess Artemis
Lest you have any doubt who Judith represents.

## Essay: On Delacroix's *The Shipwreck of Don Juan*

Delacroix, now that's one bleak take on things. My dark perspective
      Has been criticized again and again; or, never mind me
Think of a writer like Charles D'Ambrosio in *The Dead Fish Museum*
      A killer collection of short stories mostly ignored
Because he's just too damn dark. But look at you, Delacroix!

      In *The Shipwreck of Don Juan* I count twenty-four disheveled
Bodies crowded in an overloaded lifeboat surrounded by a broad
      Expanse of sea and sky: dark, cold, mercilessly endless
Sea and sky as implacable elements, neither waiting nor caring
      Merely there, indifferent to the shipwrecks' struggle.

In Byron's poem, Don Juan at least survives, swims ashore to find
      Love with beautiful, seventeen-year-old Haidée
The slave trader's vivacious daughter, and thus desire once again
      Saves us and makes a heartless world habitable.
But that bit of evasion is not for you, Delacroix, not where sea licks

      Gunwale, and the sheer strake of a fragile wooden vessel
Rides inches above turbulent waters beneath a fast-moving sky:
      Here the desperate gather in an anxious circle
One man reaches into a hat and draws out his fate as others watch
      In gaunt anticipation, fearing the sound of their name.

Because of course they're going to drink the blood and eat the flesh
      Drained and peeled from their fellow shipwrecks.
Now that's cold: an insensate universe where brutes and savages
      Will slaughter sons and daughters to hold off starvation
To survive another day where the sea roils and a bleak sky threatens.

Myself, I prefer art that's uplifting, as long as it's not the usual
Dreck: boy meets girl and lives happily ever after; kindness
        Triumphs over cruelty and avarice; decency over greed, ugliness
All manner of viciousness, of violence and human depravity—
        Because, well, that's just not true. I'm sorry. It's just not.

At the Met, I take a seat on a bench and contemplate your painting.
        It's raining outside. In here, a lifeboat full of shipwrecks
Struggles to survive. In a moment I'll get up and go find your tigers
        Those sleekly muscled hunters you obviously admire
Stretched out luxuriously on the ground, lazing under a maculate sky.

## X a Little Drunk, at 20

1.

Dazed from drink but not utterly, hopelessly drunk
      Black leather jacket with a fake fur collar pulled
Tight around his neck, X is sitting on the bottom
      Step

      Stairs leading up to his dingy, second-floor, two-room
Apartment. It's dark and late and cold and X has just come
      Back from the local bars, where others are still
         Drinking.

2.

Something about the place and the moment lodges itself in X's
      Memory: the dark of the hallway, the wind outside
Calling through cracks in the front door, the late-night
      Quiet.

      He doesn't know it yet but he will remember this moment
Forever. It's as if something essential is captured there:
      Wind, dark, cold, and X on the stairs, the world slightly
         Spinning.

3.

Forty, fifty years later he'll still see himself sitting in the dark
      Wind still rushing past the closed front door. Everything will
Change. He'll marry, have a family, divorce and marry again
      Twice.

      He'll do well in his chosen career, earn and return his family's
Love, grow into the life of a decent man—and still he'll be in that
      Hallway, as if something in that moment remains forever
         Unchanged.

# X at 70, a Walk in the Woods

1.

October's bright fires in a hush of breeze, leaf
        Flutter red and orange, patch of cloudless blue
Sky and X on a dirt trail banked with flourishing
        Sweetspire:

        Morning, bright sunlight, crisp air against skin
Knotted tree roots twisting across the trail, birds
        Screeching invisible in treetops, a murder of crows
                Cawing.

2.

Another fall morning and X alive in the heart of it. He
        Breathes deep, works bone and muscle, his arms
Swing like pendulums as he climbs a steep rise, as he
        Descends

        Winding his way around a tortuous deep wood's
Path toward a stream swollen from a recent rain
        Water rushing over stones and a fallen tree
                Branch.

3.

X stops there to sit a minute and catch his breath. He
        Takes in the noisy silence: water rush, bird-
Song, wind in leaves, and all around him the bright fall
        Eruption

        Of color: another October and X is still here, walking
Through the flaming maze of it all, the screaming
        Clamor of life's swift blaze, his stunned heart
                Swelling.

# Picture Taken on a Country Road

*for Paul*

Enigma, the inexplicable distance between this picture of you as a child
Striped tee under a zip-up sweater and your face alight with pleasure
If only the fleeting pleasure of a smile in the moment something said
A gesture by the picture-taker or a witty quip or word that surprised us
Leaning against a boxy Volvo on a country road in Rome, New York.

In order of age: you, your brother, me. I'm your uncle and the oldest.
I'm looking at you now in that grainy photograph some forty years old
A handsome boy with hair to your shoulders and a bright spontaneous smile.
Beside us beside the car, the road in sunlight a dazzled line of trees glittering.

A riddle, the distance between that moment and the last time I saw you
Days before your last day, your drug-ravaged body jittery, your face bruised
The spirit the music gone out of you, all that's left to see a wavering shell
Unsteady in the parking lot of the funeral parlor where your father lay.

You, me, and your brother leaning against a car on a pleasant day in Rome.
A mystery any bright road early in sunlight, where the glittering road goes.

## As a Storm Approaches

Birds chatter under gashes of lightning, clouds
        Tumble and rollick low and dangerous
Roiling through a seething deep-slate sky.

These last decades have been full of heartbreak.
        I don't mean us, here in the U.S., I mean the dead
In Iraq and Afghanistan, in Syria and Palestine.

I mean refugees drowning, famine and starvation.
        I mean bombings and drones, missiles and war.
There are times it feels like the whole world is burning.

What else is reasonable but to call ourselves fortunate?
        The news is full of such suffering
While we watch bright yellow forsythia bloom

In our lush green yards or the vivid pink petals
        Of a flowering cherry tree stripped by the wind
Like it's raining the sweetest, most soothing fire.

*Spring, 2018*

# X in the Tickseed

1.

There's X in his garden, on his knees, among flowering
        Plants, *coreopsis verticillata,* the whorled
Tickseed's flashy yellow petals in thick, bushy
        Clumps.

        X yanks out the stubborn crabgrass, the ground-
Clinging wild strawberries, the various hungry
        Weeds until his hands are black and dirt-
            Caked.

2.

It's midsummer and the noon sun bears down on X
        Mercilessly. He's wearing a wide-brimmed straw
Hat and knee pads, the same outfit his mother
        Wore

        When she worked in the garden. X looks up and leans
Back, remembering his mother tending to the purple
        Salvia, the careful way she snipped and pruned
            Weeds.

3.

She's been dead a dozen years and still he feels her nearby
        Presence in this sweltering day's midsummer
Heat, X on his knees among clumps of whorled
        Tickseed

        His mother on her knees tending a row of purple
Salvia, suddenly right there alongside him, near as the sun's
        Burn on his shoulders, real as the breeze ruffling his
            Hair.

# X on Fear & Joy

**1.**

X doesn't know anyone who isn't anxious at least some of the time, while
    Some are anxious most of the time, and X wonders if
"Anxiety" isn't another word for fear, for fearfulness, though spread
    Out

    Over time, generalized, an unspecified fear of the world's bared
Teeth, the way disease and death and cruelty and violence are always
    Waiting as you pick up a piece of fruit or start down
        Stairs.

**2.**

But then X doesn't know anyone who isn't joyful some of the time, while
    Some are joyful most of the time, and X wonders if
"Joy" isn't another word for wonder, for openness to wonder, though spread
    Out

    Over time, generalized, an unspecified wonder at the world's open
Arms, the way we so often sacrifice for each other, help out in hard
    Times, give what we can, all the many instances of our
        Selflessness.

**3.**

X would like to always choose joy over fear: he tries but he finds it hard
    Work. The way sunlight filters through a canopy of trees or
Sets the late-evening fields on fire, the way the ocean beckons and waves
    Roar

    Or the long river of bodies flows along a crowded city street, the
Chatter of language, the touch and swell—X wants it all to go on
    Forever and he knows it won't. He chooses joy but it's still a
        Struggle.

## A Few Words to a Young American Killed in the Tet Offensive

Here is a field in Vietnam where I didn't die
      Alongside what remains of the Quang Tri Citadel
The smell of ordnance in a warm breeze
      The crush of bombs and sear of fire:
Where young men looked a last time at a burning sky
      In the maze of their lives reached a blind corner
So many miles from their homes
                    Where I played
      In a mountain waterfall with sun on my face
Where I danced to the ecstatic music of the time—
      the Beatles, the Stones, the Youngbloods, the Who—
Danced and flashed the peace sign stoned out of my mind
      While others bled curled up in pain
As sound bleached out and the last light faded from their eyes.


      It embarrasses me now to think back on what I believed then:
In a coming age of peace and harmony in universal
      Brother- and sisterhood in no more war in sexual freedom
In drugs that might bring us closer to God
      In a coming revolution in a return to the land in chants
In the power of the people and the uprising of love.
                    We were fools.
      But we were young and we believed—
Before Afghanistan and Iraq and our endless wars.
      This was Vietnam where you died in a bloody offensive
While I marched against the war and danced
      In fields lit up with bonfires
                And learned a few chords on the guitar.
We were both of us doing what we were told
      Only listening to different voices.
              One set commanded
Duty and you offered up your life in a burning field.
      Another set demanded rebellion

And I lived on to see more wars
                        More corruption
                                        History repeated
            Till it feels to me now as if none of it mattered.


You remain in a green field beside the Quang Tri Citadel.
            I'm in a quiet house looking out over mountains.
I was able to change nothing. As were you. And I'm sorry
            For us all, but especially for your suffering and your loss
Which I've imagined repeatedly over the years with sadness
            With the wish I could explain that I believed
It might be different.
                        We were so young. Both of us
            Doing what we were told was right
Neither of us changing anything
            Beyond the direction and duration of our lives.

# Essay: On Frank O'Connor's "Guests of the Nation"

It's the ending that crushes me with every reading: after the Irishman
   Donovan executes Hawkins and Belcher, his British prisoners,
The narrator, Bonaparte, tells the reader that anything that happened
   After that night in the bog, after shooting those British
Boys they had been holding captive for many months
   And with whom they had become friends, after their bodies
Lay stiffening in the lantern-lit patch of muck and ageless bog
   "Anything that happened to me afterwards,
I never felt the same about again."

Days earlier, the British had executed four Irish prisoners, one of them
   A boy of sixteen, and so the Irish ordered Hawkins
And Belcher executed in return. This was the 1919 Anglo-Irish War
   Or the Irish War of Independence. Bonaparte was fighting
For a free Ireland. Had he refused the order he would have
   Likely been executed as a traitor. Sympathetic as I am to Bonaparte
Who comes across as a decent man and who argued hard
   Against the shootings, he did do his part
And finish off Hawkins with a second bullet.

Among the several characters in the story is an old woman who keeps
   The cottage where the prisoners are being held.
She takes care of the boys and falls to her knees in prayer when she sees
   What has been done. Steeped in superstition, she is in part
A comic figure. She blames the long drought on Jupiter Pluvius
   And World War I on "the Italian count that stole
The heathen divinity out of the temple in Japan," reasoning
   That "nothing but sorrow and want can follow the people
That disturb the hidden powers."

I can't say why this story affects me so deeply. I came of age during
   The Vietnam War and resisted the draft; then I pulled
A high number in the lottery and never served. I knew
   The war poetry of Wilfred Owen and Rupert Brooke.

I had Owen's "Dulce et Decorum Est" memorized. I had read
  Remarque's *All Quiet on the Western Front,* Trumbo's *Johnny*
*Got His Gun,* and Heller's *Catch-22.* I listened to Dylan sing Seeger's
  "Where Have All the Flower Gone," and Country Joe and the Fish
Perform their antiwar "Vietnam Song" at Woodstock.

There's something of that in my response to "Guests of the Nation."
  Something of the sorrow I feel for all who died
In Vietnam, and my refusal to be among them
  A refusal that altered the course of my life and possibly condemned
Someone else to die in my place. That thought is always with me
  But there's something more, something that shatters
When I read those closing lines and see Bonaparte out there in the night
  Bog, where "it was all mad lonely with nothing but a patch
Of lantern-light between ourselves and the dark."

When I see those boys bleeding out in the muck, and the gun in Bonaparte's
  Hand, within me something falls apart. It's war itself I think
That rattles me, the fact of it from which there appears to be no escape.
  I see bodies slowly sinking, a gun in someone's hand the moment
After a choice has been made, when a heartbroken old woman falls
  To her knees in a cottage and prays in the dying light
To the hidden powers, and all things are forever altered, disrupted
  On into the future, unending, the bodies always falling
And nothing ever the same.

# X's Shocked Heart

1.

Shithead, you must be the devil's origin
     The way you talk so miserable at times
Busting into whatever X might be
     Thinking.

     Lurking in the back of his mind
Voice for everything unspeakably
     Ugly, conduit for all things
          Vile.

2.

X calls you "Evilhead," "Shithead," "Uglyhead"
     Ignores the nasty crap you utter, shuts you
Down, and still you skulk anonymous in the dark
     Waiting.

     Speaker for the opposite of what is good or just
Spokesthing for what shouldn't be spoken, shouter
     Out of the sludge, out of the foul excremental
          Muck.

3.

Voice of the devil, or the origin of the devil
     Myth, fetid aspect of mind that shouts out
Counters good with bad, speaks up for all things
     Wrong.

     Nothing is too horrid to be conjured, spelled
Out, leaving the shocked heart ashamed, X
     Appalled that such a voice is his and unbidden
          Speaks.

# X & Snow

1.

Here in the mountains where X lives, snow falls
      Gently this morning, white flakes delicately
Drifting out of a slate-blue sky, while the great
      Pines

      Dip their long green boughs earthward to cast
Off weather's slight burden, and the hush of snow-
      Fall quiets even the traffic from distant
          Roads.

2.

This world is awash in the great beauty of God: X doesn't
      Dismiss that. He never has. Under this snowfall
Somewhere a man presses a loaded gun to his heart, a woman
      Screams

      For help, a torturer puts a black hood over someone's
Head, a soldier laughs as he cuts a boy's throat. Under this
      Gorgeous morning sky multitudes cower and
          Suffer.

3.

X is out in the weather looking up at the blue sky: fat snowflakes
      Stick to his hair. How to reconcile one with the other
Beauty and terror, a child dying and a woman holding her
      Healthy

      Child to her breast, the great light of God's love in their
Eyes? X sticks out his tongue as if he might swallow the sky
      Whole, take it inside him, vast and unthinking and without
          Doubt.

## Essay: On Edgar Allan Poe

In every story someone is buried alive: in dungeons, pits
      Maelstroms, caves—always the terrifying
Descent. In one such tale a fisherman's hair goes glistening
      White from sable black overnight: he's
Been pushed into a whirlpool that pulls him fathoms
      Deep beneath the ocean's turbulent surface.

Buried under the sea with craggy rocks below and a black sky
      Above, the fisherman gives up hope of survival
Finds peace enough to observe the elements' frightful power.
      He survives thanks to the careful ratiocination
Poe extols most entertainingly in his detective fiction, the very
      Reasoning Sir Arthur Conan Doyle pilfered

And made more famous in his Sherlock Holmes tales. Poe
      The trenchant literary critic argues meaning
In fiction should always travel beneath the story's surface: thus
      The maelstrom that swallows the fisherman
Is not only a maelstrom. It is also the swirling psyche threatening
      Oblivion, overwhelming, devouring, destroying

Pulling us down onto razor-sharp rocks that will shred to nothing
      Whatever bits of coherence make life bearable—
Or even for some, beautiful. Poe struggled. He drank, he gambled
      He died muttering on a Baltimore street corner.
"The Raven" is the poem that made him famous, though his
      Reputation rests not on his poetry but his fiction

Where he is credited with inventing the modern short story.
      It is in his fiction, in entertaining story after
Entertaining story, that he takes us down into one terrifying abyss
      Or another and reads out for us what he finds there.
In "The Raven," after he hears that gentle tapping, it's late at night
      Before he has the courage to open his chamber door.

What he sees there is darkness and nothing more. That's what
        Makes him Edgar Allan Poe. It's a vision that still
Haunts. Darkness is all he sees: "Darkness there and nothing more."

## Essay: On Tolstoy's "The Death of Ivan Ilyich"

When I was young, I reread Tolstoy's "The Death of Ivan Ilyich"
   Every few years. I found in the story a message about how
To live one's life that I didn't want to forget. The theme is hardly
   Original, now or then: Tolstoy reminds his readers that death
Is inevitable and unpredictable. It may come at any time.
   Thus, to lead one's life in pursuit of decorum and status
All of which will come to nothing in the end, is a terrible abnegation
   Of life's great challenge: to figure out how to live
With the fact of your own death.

When I was young, my generation dreamed of a world without wars
   And endless violence. We marched in the streets and resisted
The draft, refusing to fight in the latest war. We said "Peace
   Brother," when we greeted each other with two fingers
Raised in a V. We believed in a coming age of peace and love:
   "This is the dawning," we sang, "of the Age of Aquarius," when
"Peace will guide the planets / And love will steer the stars."
   A half million of us gathered at Woodstock, a music festival
Billed as "an Aquarian Exposition."

When I was young, "The Death of Ivan Ilyich" gave me permission
   To break traditions: I wouldn't cross oceans to fight in a war
As all my uncles had before me; I wouldn't die in a village where
   I couldn't speak the language, as my oldest uncle had, the one
I was named for, killed in France soon after the Normandy invasion;
   I wouldn't marry to be respectable and settle down to raise a family
As Ivan Ilyich had; I wouldn't live subject to convention and custom;
   I would "fly my freak flag high," as we said in those
Heady days of resistance and rebellion.

When I was young, the world seemed full of possibility: we could be better
   As a species; we could love one another, behave with humility
Respect the planet and live closer to the land—and that's what I gleaned
   From Tolstoy's great novella, "The Death of Ivan Ilyich." To resist

Convention; to live with goodwill and generosity; to be like the peasant
   Gerasim, who, when Ivan Ilyich was uncomfortable, would hold
His master's legs on his shoulders throughout the long night to provide
   The man a little relief from the debilitating pain
That was slowing eating away his life.

Now that I'm old, I see that though I thought I understood the story's principal
   Theme, really I only took from it what I needed: permission to rebel against
A repressive culture, as the young typically do from generation to generation. Ivan
   Ilyich suffers terribly before his death. For three days he screams in agony
And this torment I took as the pain necessary to reveal at last how he misused
   His only life. I was young and I couldn't yet see suffering as purification
As the burning away of this life's dreams and illusions, till all that's left is death's
   Final grace and redemption. Now that I'm old and living in an age of endless
Wars; now as the planet withers all around me and species

One by one tumble into extinction; now I imagine Tolstoy's arm around my
   Shoulder, offering me something to hold onto, a faith and a consolation.

# X & the Exigencies of Daily Life

1.

Socks; slippers; a ratty, old, red terrycloth robe X loves:
     Getting out of bed, throwing on some clothes, turning
Up the thermostat, a quick email and news check before
     Breakfast.

     The daily morning prayers for his daughter, for his family
Friends and loved ones, for himself, for guidance in a world
     Ultimately unknowable, offering love and gratitude, offering
         Thanks.

2.

Once each day a walk in the company of trees, grasses, streams, fields
     Birds that sing in quick bursts or the ever-present crows cawing
Calling out to each other whatever it is they have to say about this
     World.

     The arm swing, the footfall, the burn in the calves climbing a steep
Hill, the burn in the lungs, the sweet pain that ceases as the heartbeat
     Slows at the top of a rise, the view of the valley, that wide green
         Expanse.

3.

What may come at any moment to put an end to it all: a vessel in the brain
     Bursts, a blockage of blood to the heart, a virus clinging to the
Lungs, a mutiny of cells, an accident like slipping in the tub or falling down
     Stairs.

     Anything. Any moment. Anywhere. Simple as putting on a robe, eating
Breakfast, taking a walk in the mountains or through fields; the Always
     Always shimmering just beside the dazzling scrim of X's everyday
         Life.

## X's Relationship to Prayer

1.

X wakes in the morning with a headache
  After a restless night of dream-filled sleep.
He stumbles to the long kitchen window's
  Sunlight.

  He leans against the sun-warmed sink
Closes his eyes, bows his head and prays
  For his daughter, his lover, his family
   Himself.

2.

All night X dreamed in muck and sludge
  He no longer bothers to remember. He's had
Enough of memories twisted into shadowy
  Scenes

  Of chaos, of danger, of worlds morbid
Obscene, submerged in the murk of urges unbound
  Dragging the sleeping body down in the heart's
   Mud.

3.

In the warmth of morning sunlight X waits
  Head bowed, for the shade to dissipate
For the fog to lift, for his body to shake off
  Sleep.

  This is the world of light where he lives
Where the garden beyond the kitchen window
  Flowers, where the body wakes and, waking,
   Prays.

## Amazing Machine the Body

Starlit, windswept. The body's antennae: sea salt, ocean spray, a gull scream overhead, a pelican dive. The body wants food: salmon clouds on sheets of slate, seafoam, spindrift.

Newly hatched sea turtles scramble for the protection of the ocean where if they survive the night they may live a hundred years.

The body rain washed, sun soaked. Feed it touch feed it fear feed it need. The body urges and dissuades. Feed it skin feed it lips and tongue, moonlight and starlight, bright sun.

Morning walks through wooded trails, city streets, village roads, along the packed sand at the shore. The body absorbs light.

Feed it battles feed it sorrow and grief. Feed it rage. The body absorbs darkness and shadow.

The white body sliding out from between navy-blue sheets.

The black body emerging from an eggshell-white comforter.

The body protects in the dark and opens in the light. Feed it knowledge feed it meaning feed it ways to move through the world.

Children scramble in awkward bodies toward touch toward sorrow where if they survive the night they may live a hundred years.

The sky darkening before a storm. The sun emerging. The body swallows, swells, rises and descends, gropes and embraces.

Starlit. Windswept.

# In the Kentucky Mountains

This is where I came around a curve
    Found black water pooled
        Where the road dipped, blacktop disappeared
The moon rose
    Its pale white reflection
        Flashing on the surface of the water.

This is where I tried to drive through water
    Only to discover its depths
        My car floating seaworthy as a boat
Before water found its way through
    Dark and cold and quickly rising
        Above the dashboard to the windows.

This is where my car turned a slow circle
    Under fast-moving clouds
        Where I rolled down my window
Climbed onto the roof
    Where I waited wet and cold
        Surrounded by mountains and woods.

I thought myself fully alone
    Marooned and slowly sinking
        When I fell back to see the stars overhead
Blink between clouds
    The moon peek and disappear
        Black water rush to the tree line:

Before three swinging lights appeared
    As if among the constellations
        Before they turned out to be oil lanterns
Descending a steep hillside
    The gait of those who carried them
        Measuring their sweep and swing.

Before a family who lived in a nearby cabin
    Threw me a braided rope
        Before they hauled me out of water
Onto the blacktop road
    Before they swaddled me in a coarse blanket
        And took me into their home.

This is where they fed me hot milk and honey
    Found me dry clothes
        Where they made me a pallet
And this is where I slept the long night
    Before they drove me to town
        On a morning streaming bright sunlight.

This is where we live.
    In just such a world.
        This, too.

## An Alphabet of Things

ARCTIC

Region of extreme cold
          At the top of the world;
After the revelation, the eyes' flat
          Gaze.


          Fingertips on the skin of someone
Loved laid out in a casket;
          White moon in the crux of
                    Winter.


BIRDSONG

Ripples and trills, unquiets
          An interior lake's unsounded depths
Out of which rises a responding
          Note.


          Call-and-response
Fluttering eruption of color
          As sound, a green
                    Cascade.


CHINE

Backbone or spine; in butchering
          To sever the backbone of an animal;
A ridge, a crest of land; a kind of
          Fabric.


          The spine of a West Virginia mountain
Severed to rip out black coal, to cut away
          Its shimmering green coat, to
                    Kill

DUSK

Twilight; darkening sky; oncoming night
        When objects fade and perspective fails
An erasure, a closing down, a swallowing, an
        Etiolation.


        An old woman's eyes hours from her
Death: blind and searching, as if exploring
        A miraculous terrain out of the dark
                Emerging.


ECDYSIS

The shedding of an outer integument
        As a layer of skin or shell, the process
Of separation: think snakes, crabs
        Cicadas.


        Going through the bookcases
Packing some in boxes by the door
        Taking art down from the walls:
                Dividing.


FICTION

Invention; a work of the imagination
        Often a literary construction, as in a poem, a play
Or a novel. A story. A thing that didn't actually
        Happen.


        That you have arrived at your success by hard work
That your failure was ordained, that you treat all
        Equally, that your partner is your one true love.
                Everything.

GUFF

Insolent back talk; empty, nonsensical, annoying
        Defiance; vexatious bullshit: as in, *I've had enough of your guff!*
Or, *That's a lot of guff!* Typical of teens wrestling with ungrounded
        Discontent.


        Shaking your fist at a wolf moon and another day of snow;
Cursing the enduring heat of a torrid summer; bemoaning
        The unearned success of undeserving
                Others.


HYPOCORISM

A pet name or term of endearment:
        "Sweetheart," "Pumpkin," "Love," "Honey"
"Bae" (which is also Danish for
        "Poop"


        And "Bye" in Icelandic). Ah, Babe
Let us be sweetie-pies forever, you
        Cutie, you schmoopy, my
                Darlin.'


INQUILINE

A species that lives commensally
        In the habitat of another species
As a pea crab thrives in an oyster
        Shell.


        My moodiness, my self-protective
Cynicism; your openness, your
        Vulnerability, your bared
                Heart.

## JE NE SAIS QUOI

A quality that distinguishes while remaining
        Indefinable. A certain *I don't know what*
That makes something extraordinary, utterly
        One.

        The slant of evening light in winter
Mist rising at dawn off a silent pond
        The way you smile when you're feeling
        Cheeky.

## KISS

The pressing together of mouth and lips
        The tongue hungry for a taste of death
The infinite not of space where stars
        Burn.

        The body dissolves in a burst of light
A flare somewhere in the endless
        Radiant in the endless
            Night.

## LUCK

The flux of chance for good or ill
        A tide that uplifts or drowns
The particular turn of mind with which you're
        Born:

        The voice that whispers love
Or fear, the way shadows traverse
        The night like gods or
            Demons.

MAGIC

The art of invoking supernatural forces
        To exert control over the things of this world;
To make objects appear or disappear, rise or
        Fall.


        A few words in a poem and the universe
Shifts; a fiction that changes you forever;
        A painting, a sculpture, a melody, a
                Psalm.


NIMIETY

A surfeit or excess, an overabundance
        As in a bountiful harvest, a plentiful yield
As in "my cup runneth over," as in no end
        Of.


        The movement of an ocean's waters over
Sand, the leap of wind through a valley
        The slow fade of night into morning
                Light.


OBLIVESCENCE

The process of forgetting; the flickering
        Disappearance into oblivion, into the
Realm of nothingness, into the forever
        Gone.


        Every dream, every moment of every day
Every touch, even the most intimate touch
        Drifting into the unbounded
                _____.

PRAYER

A sincere petition to or request made of
  God; a formal incantation of praise or
Adoration offered, again, to God; a
  Supplication.

  A whispered cry in the storm, a calling
Out, a word with the endless, on hands and
  Knees, a beseeching, an appeal, a
    Plea.


QUEST

The act of seeking; a search; in medieval
  Romance, a knight's road trip and performance
Of prescribed feats on the way to a desired
  Goal.

  To stay the beast, to step out of, to be free of, to open
Up, to walk through, to see, to flame, to incandesce
  As a wildfire races, as the skies open, as lightning
    Sizzles.


RACONTEUSE

A woman skilled at telling stories
  At weaving engaging narratives
A tale-teller, a word-slinger, a spell-
  Binder.

  Dorothy Parker at the Algonquin
Beejay Silcox in my living room
  Woman on a Sunday porch letting
    Loose.

SAPIOSEXUAL

One who finds intelligence to be sexually
          Arousing; one pulled toward intimacy
By the lucid expression of a complex
          Idea.

          When she talks brilliantly about the Sixth
Extinction (or anything, really) he winds up imagining
          Sex. He's hopeless. He can't help it. He's
                    Sorry.


TURPITUDE

Depravity; shameful behavior; often used in
          Conjunction with "moral," suggesting conduct
Contrary to commonly held standards of
          Decency.

          As in sexual assault; as in habitual lying; as in
Supporting racism, xenophobia, misogyny; as in
          Ripping children from their mothers'
                    Arms.


UBIQUITY

Being everywhere at once, at the same time:
          Omnipresence, for example, the majesty
Of God. All-presence. Everywhereness.
          Universality.

          The dreams of sleepers comingling with
The One, the field that carries every
          Breath, the notes that sound one
                    Chord.

VACUITY

Lacking content; emptiness; the state of being
        Without, devoid, vacant, blank.
Often used to suggest absence of substantive
        Thought.


        The instant before an orgasm and not
The moments after. Deep space and the space within
        That closes down, the impenetrable
                Heart.


WARRIOR

A fighter; one who engages in battle;
        A devotee of war; an instrument of armed
Conflict; a bloodletter, a destroyer, a
        Killer.


        To be a warrior requires an opposing
Warrior. Otherwise, you're merely a
        Murderer. Hatred is useful, whipped-up
                Enmity.


XENOPHOBE

Someone who mocks or hates difference:
        Skin color, religion, customs, manners, dress
Anything other than what's known, what's
        Habituated.


        Sets fire to a mosque, a temple, a Catholic
Church; knocks over headstones in a Jewish
        Cemetery; beats a gay man, lives in
                Fear.

YEARNER

One who yearns, aches, pines, hungers, thirsts
        After; one who desires and who
Has not achieved the object of
        Desire.

        To wish this world other than
Endless violence, perpetual war
        Bombs, massacres, rapes
                Murder.


ZAPPER

One who zaps, maligns, slanders
        Censors: a nagger, a nitpicker
A carper, a complainer, a creepy
        Critic.

        The difficult poem you worked on forever
Rejected. The novel you slaved over, turned
        Down. Dream mocker, wish
                Slaughterer.

# X & His Family

1.

Early morning and a bird he can't see outside his window
      Taps at the glass, intent on disturbing X's
Sleep. He opens his eyes to a familiar room in dawn's bluish
      Light.

      His brother's sculpture is on a table beside his bed;
Two tapestries woven by his mother hang from a side
      Wall; directly across from X, a pair of his father's
        Oils.

2.

X's girlfriend calls his bedroom the museum of the beloved
      Dead. X can't argue. He sleeps each night
Surrounded by the works of their hands, his spirited
      Family.

      When he wakes each day it's as if they're still with him:
Mother at the kitchen table, railing against this or that; Father
      Arguing with her; X and his brother taking it all
        In.

3.

The unseen bird taps at the window glass. It's as if someone's
      Knocking at a door, persistent, intent on awakening X's
Attention. On the other side of the window is the glistening
      World

      Birds and grass, rough breezes and the tall trees' wavering
Crowns. The bird taps and taps, calling X up from sleep
      Calling him away from his bed, calling him out to the waiting
      Day.

# X & Nick Cave

1.

An old woman has fallen asleep in a Brooklyn subway
      Station. She's nicely dressed in black slacks and a white
Blouse. At the other end of the platform a pair of young
      Musicians

      Play Nick Cave's "Into My Arms" on neon-green electric
Cellos. It's late. The station is sparsely populated. Maybe five
      People in addition to X are standing around
           Waiting.

2.

The old woman's head has fallen forward so that her thinning
      Hair has come undone, exposing a gray and crusty
Bald spot crossed with the thin red lines of several
      Scratches.

      When X sits alongside her and taps her on the shoulder, she
Looks up, startled. X smiles his warmest smile
      Apologizes for disturbing her, and politely asks for
           Directions.

3.

The old woman answers as she fixes her hair and straightens her
      Blouse. She tells him to take the L to Union
Square, and she returns his smile. X thanks her and moves
      Away.

      The musicians on the other end of the platform are very
Young, maybe not yet even out of their teens. The Nick Cave
      Song's refrain is "Into my arms, O Lord / Into my
           Arms."

# Three Views of a Lake

1.

Body of water where a child has gone
      Missing, where bathers in a line
Search step-by-step, wading through
      Mire.

      Mouth reflecting a cobalt-blue
Sky. Maw of Nothing, swallowing a child
      Whole. Craw of a baffling
         God.

2.

Body of water raucous with children
      Swimming, where a field of hungry bodies
Bathe in the heat of a brilliant late-morning
      Sun.

      Mirror of a powder-blue sky, dazzling
Sunlight skittering across the surface of its glacial
      Depths, emerald-green spaces of shimmering
      Light.

3.

The surface of the earth under a retreating glacier
      Eroded, an excavated emptiness, cavernous
Deep, a gaping hole filled with a flood of icy
      Melt.

      Body of water under sun under cloud under
Sky, body of water where life scurries and slithers
      Fish in its murky depths, plankton and weed
      Silt.

# Narcissus

Bright yellow star flowers of early spring
        Spring up on my lawn so long unmown
           It's morphing
Back into the mountain meadow it used to be
        Before someone unknown
           A few generations ago
Built this house where I've lived alone for years.

        It's quiet here. Next lot over
           There are horses and goats.
I like to listen when the horses gallop side-by-side
        Or when goats bleat and squeal
           Making a racket
That I nonetheless think of as quiet
        A boy who grew up in a city full of cars and planes
           Upstairs neighbors threatening
To take each others' lives.

        Such fury those childhood years
           Much of it unseen.

It's in the amaryllis family, the yellow star flower
        As is the narcissus of Europe and the spider lily.
           Thinking of Narcissus, you know it was quiet
Where he gazed upon himself looking up
        From under still water.
           In Caravaggio's painting
Narcissus's eyes are dark
        As he peers down at his shadowy double
           His right hand immersed in black water
Up to his dirt-smudged wrist.
        There must be animals around as he ponders
           That still pond where a murky self looks back

But Caravaggio's brush has blackened all that out:
Flowers, animals, trees, weather
All the stuff of the world.
There's nothing anywhere to distract him
Not goats or horses or bright flowers.
His parted lips suggest desire.
He's intent, contemplating this blurred likeness of himself
And I know we're supposed to have the myth in mind
Narcissus in love with his own appearance
But if we didn't know the story, if no one had ever told us
We'd see a man absorbed in contemplating
His shadowy reflection, wondering what that dark
Fellow knows that he doesn't, perhaps.
Or imagining a story to explain such separation.
And maybe longing for reconciliation with that other
Study of himself that he can't quite see clearly
But clearly sees just under water
Where it rose up from the bottom to meet him
The world blacked out the way it is when bodies meet
Lean close and move in
For that first, dangerous kiss.

# X & Night

1.

After sunlight fades to dusk and the moon
      Rises over rustling trees, empty gravel
Roads, and the porch light of a neighbor's
      House

      X walks barefoot in the dark yard's
Shadows. It's summer and the warm
      Grass and a chattering breeze
          Comfort.

2.

After the long day plays out its troubled
      Hand, after X finds himself again
Busted, he wanders through his yard's dark
      Corners.

      This world, to be inherited by no one
Nonetheless presses and demands, pushes
      Cajoles, harasses, deals out repeated
          Sorrows.

3.

Overhead the black sky's flickering web of stars
      Quakes as if touched by an unseen
Hand and the moon cuts a pale bright
      Circle

      Out of the dark. X lies down and looks
Up into the endless, into the inky silk
      Black of forever, into the long night's
          Embrace.

# X & Wind

1.

The summer morning breeze that adores
      Skin; the long night's sustained whispering . . .
X has a thing with wind, a shockingly libidinous
      Affair.

      It's lascivious, the wind, with its probing
Fingers brushing back his hair, reaching
      Under his clothes, massaging him
            Everywhere.

2.

Nights at the shore, under stars, beside the talkative
      Ocean, X has walked alone, barely clothed, wind
Hungry all over him, brushing his lips, sweeping
      Sand

      Off the beach to pelt his skin teasingly
Gently, with just enough sting to awaken
      Desire, to arouse the body with its intimate
            Kiss.

3.

X understands the need to be careful, to maintain
      Control, to not let things get out of hand. He
Knows what can happen if the wind blows up
      Rages:

      It can tear down neighborhoods, destroy every
Edifice. He knows the wind can be an irrational, dangerous
      Lover, and still he can never resist its awakening
            Touch.

# Three Thoughts on the Summer of 2020

### 1. MEN WITH GUNS

Guard statues of men with guns
Guns held lovingly one hand
Cradles the forestock the butt
Snug against hip the barrel
Pointed at clouds above throngs
Mostly young women and men
Children too children with mothers
Children in strollers with fathers
Men with guns wear camo more guns
Strapped to hips guard statues of men
Swords drawn on horseback blades
Pointed to clouds while the throng
Chants spray-paints listens to speeches
Prays calls out the names of the dead
Sings the silenced names the murdered
The slaughtered the maimed faces down
Men with guns guarding statues of men
Swords raised guns readied glistening
Bronze and shimmering awaiting a future
Men with guns cannot hold off a future
That will tear them down.

### 2. MASKS

That speak say I Can't Breathe say Vote
Say Take It to the Streets say Heroes Work Here
Say Smile say We Will Beat This say Nasty Women
Say Stay Home say Biden 2020 say Black Lives
Matter say Fuck Trump say White Silence
Equals White Violence say Vote Blue No Matter
Who say Remember in November say
Speak the Names as tear gas canisters
As flash-bangs as batons fists shields helmets

Say silence say compliance say bodies pushed
Heads cracked open two black men found
Hanged in public places ruled suicides
Under masks mouths sick of the same
Again choking again shooting beating
Say sick of it say white and black sick of it
Say change, change, change, change, change.

## 3. ISOLATION

Summer of the pandemic summer of stay home
Turns out Oreo fudge-dipped mint crème cookies
Sales soared along with fig Newtons and Nutter
Butters as we grazed our kitchens for relief for
Comfort locked-in with the endless silence turns
Out we'd been avoiding all along the night hum
Rain patter wind song of nothing the oceanic
Note of forever sounding through the hall
Filling the bedroom's nightscape whispering
Our names.

## Accidents

Backing out of his spot in the nearly always empty
      Parking lot, X stops to check the rearview mirror
            Where two young women in jeans

Sit cross-legged on the ground.
      Had he gone another few feet
            He would have run them down.

When he was in his twenties
      He drove a flashy, chartreuse Fiat Spider
            A sleek machine, appropriate for his age

As was the frequent late-night carousing. Once
      When driving tired he shifted out of consciousness
            From the right lane to the left

Awakened beside an eighteen-wheeler broken down
      A big rig, lifted on monster wheels
            High off the ground.

The collision would have decapitated him
      Had he not in his sleep switched lanes.
            Now two young women in jeans

Hold hands as they leave a nearly empty parking lot
      Where alone behind the wheel of his car
            He bows his head and briefly prays.

# Three Transmutations of a Memory

1.

*After Christmas, Brooklyn, Night*

In an abandoned lot gathered Christmas trees are set on fire.
      Older boys swing a younger boy toward flames.
Overhead, stars flicker through a smoky haze and the boy
      Screams.

      Heat pushes against his face. His hair is singed. In the blazing
Night, he's transformed. Look! Look! How high the flames
      Leap! How the trees explode and roar! How the night
         Burns!

2.

*Boy, After the Holidays*

In the lot where they gathered discarded Christmas
      Trees and set them ablaze, the towering big boys
Swung him toward the fire, where shrieking angels
      Seethed.

      Holy voices crackled in his ears, wailed beneath
Stars dim in a smoky haze, while the big boys
      Danced like dervishes, their laughter echoing
         Prayers.

3.

*Where He Finds Revelations*

In the black hollows of the heart, where the dark animals
      Reign, where keening rises up like lamentations
Whipped and fretted until a sleek skin sheer as a birth caul
      Bursts.

Light pierces smoke and shadow as injured creatures
Scatter in the presence of what emerges blazing to reveal
     Boys as towering angels, the fire their frenzied ecstatic
     Song.

# X & Music

1.

First, jazz: X's big brother a musician, a drummer
      Drum set taking up two-thirds of his bedroom.
He played along to jazz and the big bands: Glenn
      Miller

      Benny Goodman, Duke Ellington, Count Basie. He
Loved Ella Fitzgerald, Sarah Vaughan, Billie Holiday. X
      Still a kid, listened on the other side of the bedroom
         Wall.

2.

Then, folk: Bob Dylan, Pete Seeger, Joan Baez, Phil Ochs.
      Graduating to blues: John Lee Hooker, Lead
Belly, Howlin' Wolf; and on to the great jazz masters: Miles
      Davis

      John Coltrane, Thelonious Monk, Bird. Thereafter an
Eclectic mix, leaning always toward jazz: Roland Kirk, the great Wayne
      Shorter, the indomitable Charles Lloyd—but also Frank
         Zappa.

3.

And all along, the subtle music of words: from Emily Dickinson
      To Ted Roethke, from Shakespeare to Mamet.
The song of language arranged as music in the end X's great
      Love.

      So many singers, so many songs! In every language, every
Medium, every culture, voices raised in celebration, sorrow
      Joy, grief, love, fear—always, even with death at the door,
         Singing!

# X & the Seasons

1.

*X, from His Teens through His Thirties*

Yes to spring's reckless slash of color and yes to summer's
  Heat and shameless swaths of flowers' wanton preening;
Yes to fall's bright death announcements scattered
  Everywhere

  Even to winter's white fist battering locked doors
Yes. Bring it all, bring it, X revels in the season's
  Provocations, in blazing heat and body-numbing
   Cold

2.

*X, from His Forties through His Sixties*

X is still in love with the world but often now he worries:
  Time moves like a magician getting from here to there
Faster than can be reasonably possible. It makes no sense how
  Fast

  Time goes, pulling the hesitant body along without
Consent, dragging it mumbling through each swift
  Season, as if X is cannonballing in free fall through
   Time.

3.

*X, in His Seventies*

Yes again—because it's clear there's nothing anywhere to grasp
  Nothing to break winter's grip, never has been
Anything to slow the turning after luxuriant summer's impulsive
  Heat

To hold off winter's final push before it all begins again—
Though in the beginning again is the spectacle and the marvel
Fiery as ever. So yes, he'll speak in wild favor and go out
Testifying.

# NOTES

## Page 12: "Essay: On Jay DeFeo's *The Rose*"

Bruce Conner's thoughts about Jay DeFeo and *The Rose* are derived from the San Francisco MOMA video, "Jay DeFeo's *The Rose:* The Enormous Painting That Was 'Almost Alive.'" I found the video online at: https://bit.ly/3pPHP77.

In the penultimate stanza, the lines spoken by Jay DeFeo, as told to Leah Levy, are taken from Pierce Jackson's video for the Whitney Museum of American Art, "Jay DeFeo's *The Rose*." The video is available online at: https://bit.ly/3i00lSj.

The Fred Martin quote that ends the poem is taken from the catalog for the 1959 *Sixteen Americans* exhibit at the Museum of Modern Art. I found the catalog here: https://www.moma.org/calendar/exhibitions/2877. The Fred Martin introduction to Jay DeFeo, which contains the quote, is on page 8.

## Page 32: "Essay: On Tolstoy's 'The Death of Ivan Ilyich'"

If you were over five years old in 1969, you don't need a note to tell you that the lyrics quoted in the second stanza are from the song "Aquarius," by Gerome Ragni, James Rado, and Galt MacDermot, from *Hair: The American Tribal Love-Rock Musical.*

x x x

I'd like to thank James Long and the staff at Louisiana State University Press, as well as all of the institutions and individuals who support the Press. My shelves are full of books from LSU, and I'm grateful to be included among their authors. Thanks, also, to the editors who published many of the poems in this collection: Caroline Chavatel, *New South;* George David Clark, *32 Poems;* Mark Drew, *Gettysburg Review;* Jessica Faust, *Southern Review;* Taylor Fedorchak, *Puerto del Sol;* Robert Nazarene and James Wilson, *American Journal of Poetry;* Nathaniel Perry, *Hampden-Sydney Poetry Review;* Stephen Reichert, *Smartish Pace;* and Katherine Smith, *Potomac Review.*

As always, I'd like to thank Steve and Clorinda Gibson, who have been my friends and fellow travelers in the arts since I was a teenager.

I've been lucky enough as a teacher to work with many younger writers, all of them important to me, and I thank them for their friendship and the gift of their talent, energy, and enthusiasm.

Thanks also to my friends and family, immediate and extended, which include the many generous and gifted poets and writers I've come to know over the years, as well as the many colleagues I've worked and studied with at Syracuse University and Virginia Tech.

Finally, thanks more than I can say to Judy Bauer and Susan Falco, the two women at the heart of my life; and to Eli Nachlas and Will Stauffer Norris, two young men who make me proud to have been a small part of their lives.

Printed in the USA
CPSIA information can be obtained
at www.ICGtesting.com
CBHW030225210524
8864CB00003B/111